Table of Contents

What Are Bats?

Bats are among the world's most misunderstood creatures. Some people think they are scary, and some think they are dangerous. But in reality, bats are important and necessary animals that improve the quality of our lives.

- Bats are mammals. They are warm-blooded and have fur. They give birth to baby bats called pups that drink milk from their mothers.

- They are the only mammals that can fly.

- There are more than 1,300 species of bats in the world. They are the second most common species in the world after rodents.

Bats live everywhere except in the world's very coldest and hottest places.

web membrane

forearm

ear

thumb

knee

second finger

foot

third finger

fourth finger

fifth finger

That's Batty!

Bats are divided into two groups: megabats and microbats. Megabats—which can be huge—eat fruit. Microbats—which can be as small as a penny—eat bugs, small animals, nectar, or blood.

Why Bats Matter

Bats make the world a better place. Without them, our food supply would suffer and we would have more pests.

- A tiny microbat can eat up to 500 mosquitoes and other small bugs in an hour.

- Bats are important pollinators. Some plants, such as bananas, avocados, and mangoes, depend on bats to transfer pollen from plant to plant.

- Fruit-eating bats are like flying farmers who spread seeds in the world's rain forests, helping to sustain the **ecosystem** as humans cut down trees to develop the land.

The tree known as Africa's tree of life—the great baobab tree—would die out if bats were no longer around to pollinate it.

That's Batty!

Two 18th-century libraries in Portugal gladly house tiny bats within their bookshelves. Each night, the bats earn their keep by eating insects that destroy books.

Bat Fact or Fiction

Most people think that bats are blind or dirty or will suck your blood. Let's set the record straight.

- Maybe you've heard someone use the expression "blind as a bat." But bats actually have pretty good eyesight. Scientists believe bats see better than people at dawn and dusk.

- Bats are as fussy as cats about cleaning themselves. They lick their fur clean and use their claws to clean their ears and comb their fur.

- Only three species of bats drink blood. They like animal blood, not human blood, and they all live in Central or South America.

That's Batty!

Bats may look like rodents with wings, but their DNA shows bats are not at all related to rats or mice. They're related to primates, the group of animals that includes lemurs, monkeys, and apes.

Where Do Bats Live?

Long ago, bats could be found only in caves, but like other animals, they have **adapted** over time. They can be found in old buildings, barns, or mines. Bats look for homes in these types of places:

- Well away from predators. Bats can be eaten by birds of prey, such as owls and hawks, as well as by predators like raccoons and weasels.

- Near food and water. The availability of food and water may change with each season, forcing bats to migrate.

- Just the right temperature. Bats need warmer temperatures when raising their young but can survive in cooler temperatures when hibernating.

Humans can provide bat **habitats** by hanging bat houses in yards and in parks.

That's Batty!

Bats like to hang out under bridges. About 1.5 million bats live under the Ann W. Richards Congress Avenue Bridge in Austin, Texas, from early spring to fall. They form the country's largest urban bat **colony**.

Life as a Bat

Most bats are **nocturnal**, sleeping by day and hunting at night. Some, like us, sleep at night. They hang by their claws and sleep upside down in large groups, sometimes with thousands of bats roosting in one place.

bat claws

Special veins keep bats' blood flowing throughout their bodies so they don't get dizzy when hanging upside down.

Bats usually live up to 20 years. The longest recorded life span of a bat, however, was 41 years!

When a large colony flies out to find food, stay out of the way and cover your ears! Bats may fly right into you if you're in their way, and they can make quite a bit of noise with all their flapping!

Most bats can hibernate, or enter torpor, for as little as a few hours or for up to a month. The little brown bat takes hibernation to a new level. It can hibernate a full six months until the insects that make up its diet are plentiful again.

skin flaps

That's Batty!

Bats are the only mammals that truly fly. Some bats can fly at speeds of more than 100 miles per hour (161 kph)! Other mammals, such as flying squirrels and flying lemurs, can only glide. They ride the wind for brief distances using flaps of skin on their sides.

It's Dinnertime!

It takes a lot of energy to fly as much as bats do so they need to eat a lot! A thumb-sized little brown bat can eat up to its entire weight every night. Bats can be broken into four groups based on diet:

- **Frugivores.** These bats eat fruit and then poop seeds to help new plants grow. Without them, some crops and rain forests would suffer decline.

- **Insectivores.** Bats control pests for farmers and homeowners. Insectivores eat destructive insects such as locusts, crickets, fruit flies, gnats, beetles, and mosquitoes.

- **Carnivores.** Some bats eat lizards, frogs, rodents, birds, and fish. Some even eat other bats!

- **Nectar feeders.** Some bats eat nectar and pollen. As they move from plant to plant, they also spread pollen, which is needed so that plants can reproduce. More than 300 species of fruit rely upon bats for pollination.

Bats of all types help keep the ecosystem in balance.

ugivores

Nectar feeders

rnivores

Insectivores

That's Batty!

If you notice your hummingbird feeder emptying more quickly than usual, it may be attracting nighttime visitors. Some bats visit feeders by night and leave them dry by morning.

Echo-echo-echo-location

While bats can use their eyes to see, many also see with their large, upright ears. Using **echolocation**, bats bounce high-pitched sounds off objects and living things to help them map their surroundings and find prey.

- An average bat's call is so high that humans can't hear it.

- The echoes that come back tell the bat how large the object or living thing is and how far away it is.

- Bats can even tell exactly what kind of prey is nearby from the echoes that are returned.

Whales, dolphins, and some birds also use echolocation for hunting.

That's Batty!

It's a good thing bat calls are outside our range of hearing. Machines have measured bat calls as loud as a nearby jet engine to those animals that can hear them. In fact, bats have to tighten a muscle in their middle ears when calling to keep themselves from going deaf.

Gotta Love Guano

Bat poop, known as **guano**, is good for the environment. Guano from frugivores and insectivores is rich in nutrients and can improve soil.

- Guano can protect soil from fungus outbreaks that can destroy lawns and gardens.

- It changes soil makeup to keep away insects that can destroy plants and crops.

- Bat poop is high in potassium nitrate, also found in fertilizers, gunpowder, and explosives. In fact, guano has been used in making gunpowder.

On the Southeast Asian island of Borneo, bats roost inside a **carnivorous** plant that relies on bat guano for nutrients.

That's Batty!

The guano from insectivores sparkles from the shiny **exoskeletons** of the insects they eat. Does that make guano pretty? You decide!

Honduran White Bat

It's time to meet some of our bat friends. We'll start with one of the cutest. This snow-white flying ball of fluff weighs about as much as a nickel. Its yellow-orange ears and nose look like leaves.

- This microbat builds tents out of the leaves of a flowering plant found in Central America rain forests to protect itself from rain and predators.

- Its white coloring acts as camouflage, reflecting green as the sun shines through the leaves of their leafy homes.

- At night, the Honduran white bat forages for food. A frugivore, it eats mostly figs, but it will eat other fruits as well.

As many as 12 bats can live within a single flower tent. But these bats don't usually stay in the same tent day after day.

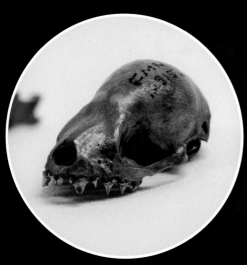

That's Batty!

A thin black layer of tissue covers the Honduran white bat's skull. Scientists believe it's a built-in natural sunscreen.

19

Big Brown Bat

The big brown bat is a microbat, though one of the larger ones with a 13-inch (33-cm) wingspan. This insectivore feasts on moths, beetles, wasps, and the very destructive corn rootworm, making it a farmer's best friend.

The big brown bat has to gain about a third of its body weight in preparation for hibernation.

Mothers raise their pups in colonies of as many as 700 bats. Males roost alone or in small groups most of the year.

Pups that fall from the roost will squeak constantly to help their mothers find them and return them safely home. Their calls can be heard for up to 30 feet (9.1 m).

Scientists have found big brown bats can hibernate for as long as 10 to 11 months at a time.

That's Batty!

Your heart probably beats between 70 and 100 times a minute. But a big brown bat's heart beats as many as 1,097 times a minute during short flights!

Giant Golden-Crowned Flying Fox

This huge megabat is the largest and among the rarest bats in the world. It's called a *flying fox* because its face looks similar to a fox's, but there's no relation between the two mammals.

- A frugivore, this bat can fly as much as 25 miles (40.2 km) in a single night in search of figs and other fruits.

- Its wingspan can reach 5.7 feet (1.7 m), nearly the size of an eagle's wingspan.

- The giant golden-crowned flying fox faces extinction from habitat loss and poaching.

This bat wraps its wings around itself like a cloak when roosting.

That's Batty!

This bat enjoys frequent baths. It uses its large wings to scoop water and pours it over its body.

Bumblebee Bat

We've met what may be the world's cutest bat. Let's meet the smallest one. The bumblebee bat, found in Thailand, weighs less than a dime. Bumblebee bats roost in groups of up to 500, keeping warm in limestone caves.

The bumblebee bat is also known as the *Kitti's hog-nosed bat* because of its hoglike snout.

It feasts mostly on flies and spiders. So if you don't like spiders, you have to be a fan of the bumblebee bat!

Tourists have been known to disturb the roosts of bumblebee bats, which is leading to their decline.

The bumblebee bat's teeny-tiny eyes are mostly hidden by its fur.

That's Batty!

If you think bumblebee bats are small, imagine the size of a baby bumblebee bat! Young pups attach themselves to their mothers when they feed to protect them from predators such as snakes, birds, cats, and squirrels.

Townsend's Big-Eared Bat

When resting, this bat curls up its long ears so they look like horns. It can point its ears forward when it flies for extra-sensitive hearing. Even though its wingspan is 12 to 13 inches (30.5 to 33 cm), it weighs only about as much as four peanuts.

This bat is found in western North America from British Columbia to Mexico. However, human activity around roosts and the use of pesticides that reduce food sources are causing a decline in the species.

The big-eared bat often hibernates in mines to stay warm, but loses its home as unused mines are sealed shut.

It can be found in forests or in desert scrub areas, where it eats mostly moths.

If a predator is nearby, colony members will cry out to one another as a warning.

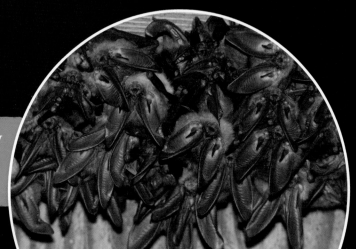

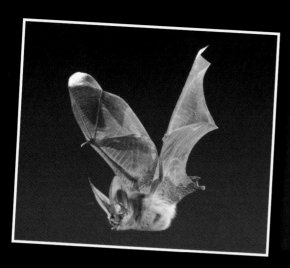

That's Batty!

The big-eared bat's appetite for moths is a big help to farmers, but this bat also helps other animals. It becomes a host to large, yellow flies, and its guano becomes food to wood rats.

Egyptian Fruit Bat

This hungry frugivore and nectar-feeder has a tiny body with a large wingspan, an almost doglike face and a long tongue. It's found in Africa and South Asia in areas where other bat species would not survive. It roosts in large colonies, staying close to one another to maintain body temperature.

This fruit bat drops fruit seeds to the ground, causing new growth. It also pollinates plants.

Farmers, however, consider it a nuisance because it eats growing crops.

Family ties are tight among Egyptian fruit bats. Mothers take excellent care of their pups, and individuals usually stay in the same colony all their lives.

Scientists consider this bat the most vocal bat of all. It's noisy!

That's Batty!

The Egyptian fruit bat makes clicking sounds much like a dolphin when using echolocation. It also makes a squeaking sound even humans can hear.

Common Vampire Bat

This tiny carnivore, which weighs less than a golf ball, is the stuff of legends. But the truth is much less exciting. Yes, the vampire bat drinks blood, and yes, it preys on sleeping creatures. But those creatures are typically cows, pigs, horses, and birds.

- Vampire bats don't usually drink human blood, but if you do get bitten by one, you will NOT turn into a vampire!

- In legends, vampire bats suck blood from their prey. But they really bite through skin and lick up the blood that comes out with their grooved tongues.

- A bat drinks only about 2 tablespoons (30 ml) of blood each night. It will share blood with a colony member that didn't find enough food that night.

A vampire bat's spit contains an enzyme that keeps blood from clotting. Scientists are studying it to see if they can use it to treat blood clots in humans.

That's Batty!

Pups get their first taste of blood at around two months old, when their mothers throw it up into their mouths. Yuck and yuck!

Mexican Free-Tailed Bat

Every night of each summer, 20 million Mexican free-tailed bats—making up the world's largest bat colony—stream out of Bracken Cave in Texas in search of mosquitoes and other insects. Farmers are grateful for the annual visitors because they eat crop-damaging pests every night.

These bats may live in large colonies, but when they hunt, it's every bat for itself. Scientists have found they can jam one another's calls when hunting by calling out when another bat closes in on prey.

These bats not only benefit crops but also human health because they eat disease-carrying insects.

Attics and old buildings are also favorite roosting sites for the Mexican free-tailed bat.

The Mexican free-tailed bat is found in North, Central, and South America and has a wingspan of about 1 foot (.3 m).

That's Batty!

Bats are lightweight, but scientists estimate the huge Texas colony weighs 270 tons (245 t). It also creates tons of guano, which becomes food to hordes of tiny organisms, beetles, and other insects.

Greater Bulldog Bat

With a wingspan of 27.5 inches (70 cm) and an orangish body, this huge bat is set apart by its unusual appearance and behavior. A carnivore, it uses echolocation to find fish that it snatches up with its long, sharp claws.

This bat has a bulldog-like snout, thick lips, and sharp fangs like a dog. No wonder it's called a *bulldog bat*!

When many fish are available, the greater bulldog bat won't bother using echolocation. Instead, it will drag its claws across the water and grab fish.

It's found in South America near bodies of water so it can have easy access to food sources.

Also known as a *greater bulldog fishing bat*, this bat's body is coated with water repellent to help it dry off quickly.

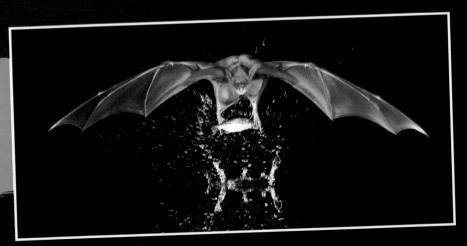

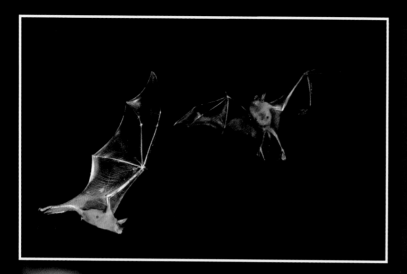

That's Batty!

This bat can either eat its prey while flying or save it for later in pouches within its expandable cheeks.

Spotted Bat

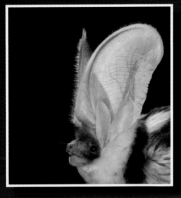

With its spotted black-and-white fur and translucent pink ears that are nearly the length of its body, this bat is among the rarest bats in North America to find because it often roosts in the crevices of cliffs.

- Unlike other bats, this insectivore likes to live alone.

- Moths are its favorite meal. But it doesn't eat the whole insect: it rips off the wings and eats only the stomach.

- The spotted bat hunts close to home and has been known to fight other bats for territory.

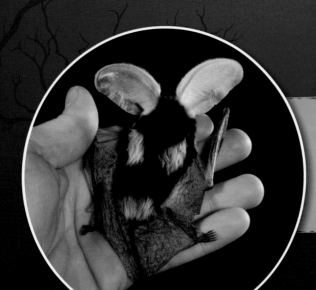

Spotted bats have been found as high as 9,842 feet (3,000 m) above sea level. Such heights provide protection from predators.

That's Batty!

This pretty bat's call is at such a low frequency that humans can hear it. It has to live in open areas so it can hear its call echoed back to it.

California Leaf-Nosed Bat

With its unusual nose and huge ears, this leaf-nosed bat is just plain funny-looking. Scientists suspect the nose shape may somehow help with echolocation, but they can't be sure.

- Its broad, short wings are designed for shorter flights. Because of its anatomy and its habitat, this bat doesn't migrate or hibernate.

- This bat is both an insectivore and a frugivore. Insects make up the bulk of its diet, but it will also eat cactus fruit.

- It's the only North American bat known to eat caterpillars.

Most bats live an average of 20 years, but this bat can live up to 30 years in the wild.

That's Batty!

This leaf-nosed bat's extra-large ears give it extra-sensitive hearing that can detect an insect's footsteps.

Lesser Long-Nosed Bat

This bat helps protect and maintain desert ecosystems by pollinating the saguaro cactus. The giant cactus is important because it provides food and nesting sites for many birds. The long-nosed bat covers its hairy face with pollen as it drinks the cactus nectar, spreading the pollen from plant to plant.

The saguaro cactus flowers open just one night a year, giving the bats a short window for pollination.

This long-nosed bat is not only a pollinator but also a frugivore. It eats cactus fruit and then helps spread the seeds through its guano.

The long-nosed bat is **endangered** as the result of loss of habitat and invasive plant species.

That's Batty!

This bat may be named for its long nose, but its tongue is even longer—about the same length as its body!

Indiana Bat

In the summer, this tiny and hungry insectivore lives under the bark of old trees near rivers and streams in the eastern United States. During the winter, it migrates north to hibernate in caves or old mines.

- This species hibernates in colonies of up to 50,000 bats to protect itself from predators.

- Humans sometimes disturb their roosts, causing decline. Habitat loss also threatens the Indiana bat's numbers.

- The use of pesticides decreases this bat's food sources.

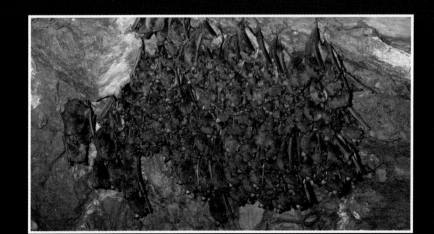

That's Batty!

Do you eat half your body weight at a meal? Probably not, but the Indiana bat does. It burns off the calories with all its flying.

Going to Bat for Bats

We've learned how bats do a world of good for the environment and even our health. But bats face many threats, putting some in danger of extinction. And without bats, we face a world of trouble.

Light pollution changes bat behavior. Large flying insects gather around lights, drawing bats away from their normal hunting grounds and affecting their diet.

Cave explorers and guano miners (yes, people who mine bat poop!) disturb roosts, causing hibernating bats to lose body fat each time and risking their starvation.

Many bats have died from white-nose syndrome, the worst wildlife disease to hit North America.

white-nose syndrome

What Can You Do?

1. Avoid caves and other roosting sites during hibernation seasons.

2. Become a bat ambassador! Tell people about the benefits of bats.

3. Put a bat house on a tree with the help of an adult, and let bats help control mosquitoes in your yard.

4. Support organizations like Bat Conservation International and the North American Society for Bat Research.

Calling All Bat Watchers

If you're becoming batty for bats, it's time to see them live and in action. Chances are excellent, if it's a warm-weather month, you can see them at one of these types of places near you:

- A bridge. Bats often roost under bridges and then come out at night to hunt.

- Near water. Bats often live near water, where they can find more flying insects.

- In forests. Bats love to roost in trees. Try visiting a local park at dusk to see the night sky come alive!

Your Best Bets for Bats

Some places are famous for the number of bats that make their homes there—places like the Ann W. Richards Congress Avenue Bridge and Bracken Cave in Texas.

Carlsbad Caverns, New Mexico

From April to October, about 1 million Mexican free-tailed bats make the caverns their home base. Bats fly out of the caverns at sunset and return between 4:00 and 6:00 a.m. The park offers a free bat information program every night from Memorial Day weekend through October.

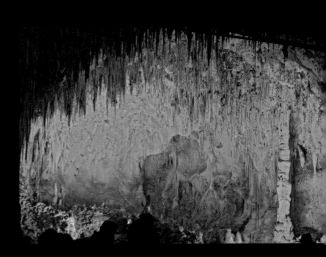

Millie Mine, Michigan

About 1 million bats of a variety of species make this mine their home from spring to early fall. The mine is gated to keep people out, but it allows bats to come and go. The best place to view the nightly display is from an observation deck uphill from the mine.

Nickajack Cave, Tennessee

Ride a canoe or kayak to a bay outside this cave on a late summer evening, and watch a colony of about 60,000 insect-eating gray bats take to the skies in search of dinner. You'll find yourself just feet away from these endangered bats as they fly right above the water in search of prey.

Glossary

adapt: change over time to help a living thing better survive in its environment

carnivorous: feeding on animals

colony: a group of animals living closely together

echolocation: the ability to bounce sound off objects and living things to find their location

ecosystem: a group of organisms and their shared environment

endangered: in danger of becoming extinct

exoskeleton: a hard, protective covering of an animal or insect

guano: bat poop

habitat: a place where a plant or animal makes its home

hibernate: spend the winter in a state of deep rest in which body functions have slowed down

light pollution: the use of artificial lights at night

mammal: a warm-blooded animal with skin or hair that gives birth to live young, which it feeds milk produced within its body

migrate: change habitats depending on the season

nocturnal: active at night

prey: an animal hunted by another animal for food

pup: baby bat

torpor: a state of remaining physically inactive

Metric Table

The metric system is a system of measurements. It is used in many parts of the world. It is also used by all scientists, no matter where they live. Here are some common abbreviations for metric measurements used in this book.

cm = centimeters
km = kilometers
kph = kilometers per hour
m = meters
ml = milliliter
t = tonnes